Elle's ABC's

A book for children

By
Elle Youn

Concept, art, design, and layout by Elle Youn

Assembly and publishing by Paper Airplane Books
www.PaperAirplaneBooks.com

Copyright 2017 by Elle Youn & Paper Airplane Books

ISBN-13: 978-0692974995

ISBN 10: 0692974997

This book in whole or parts thereof, may not be reproduced for commercial use in any form without permission in writing from the publisher, Paper Airplane Books.

Please do not participate in digital or physical piracy of any copyrighted materials. Your support of the author's rights is appreciated.

Written, Published, and Printed in the USA!

www.ingramcontent.com/pod-product-compliance
Lightning Source LLC
Chambersburg PA
CBHW041235040426
42444CB00003B/177